Praise for Susan Deborah King

"What are we to learn from the loss of loved ones, from the unspeakable tragedy of a young person's accidental gun death, from wounds that can never heal, from bombs and plagues and mass killings? Sam King, a gentle leader indeed, teaches us to plant our griefs and sorrows along with our tulip bulbs – and then to watch, wait and witness the explosion of life they hold. In these poems, she does God's work."

~ Sarah T (Sally) Williams, former book editor,
Minneapolis Star Tribune

"Bright, lively, high-powered, sensuous: Susan Deborah King's *Dropping into the Flower* is no ditzy stroll through daisies. The world's mayhem, 'hideous with grief' remains elbow-near. But King offers readers these beautifully crafted poems; they remind us that a garden's life-cycle can '…raise the alarming/ standard of love.' Her poems are allegories, metaphors, crescendos of passion, of life. They are irrepressible outbursts like the graffiti King found on the Appalachian Trail: 'I was love.' This is poetry that urges us to see that '…(to) have one's essence be/to another/(is) utterly essential…' and to live, 'as if your soul were a seed splitting open.'"

~ Sharon Chmielarz, author of *Love from the Yellowstone Trail*

Poetry Books by Susan Deborah King

Dropping Into the Flower

Bog Orchids

One-Breasted Woman

Coven (a Minnesota Book Award nominee)

Tabernacle: Poems of an Island

Dropping into the Flower

Poems by

Susan Deborah King

Susan Deborah King (handwritten signature)

For Barb + Eva,
With deep admiration
of how you walk in the world
the insight + radiance you
share. With wishes for

Holy Cow! Press | Duluth, Minnesota | 2013

full flowering & all you care about.
With love, Sam
12/13

First printing, 2013

ISBN 978-0-9859818-1-5

10 9 8 7 6 5 4 3 2 1

This project is supported in part by grant awards from the Ben and Jeanne Overman Charitable Trust, the Elmer L. and Eleanor J. Andersen Foundation, the Cy and Paula DeCosse Fund of the Minneapolis Foundation, The Lenfestey Family Foundation, and by gifts from individual donors.

Holy Cow! Press books are distributed to the trade by Consortium Book Sales & Distribution, c/o Perseus Distribution, 210 American Drive, Jackson, TN 38301.

For inquiries, please write to:
Holy Cow! Press
Post Office Box 3170, Mount Royal Station
Duluth, MN 55803

Please visit our website at www.holycowpress.org

Acknowledgements

The author would like to thank the journals
in which some of these poems appeared:

The MacGuffin:
"Haleakala"

The Minnesota Poetry Calendar:
"Ole,"
"Sonnet for February 23"

Thema: "Dreamland Café"

Castings: "Peepers"

The Willow Review:
"Flowers that are Truly Orange Are Relatively Few,"
"Driving Toward New Milford, May 1,"
"Back from the Funeral of a Twelve-Year-Old,"
"Weeds"

Potato Eyes: "Leaving"

Tar River Poetry:
"I Was Love,"
"I Really Want to Know"

Avocet: "Again"

Albatross: "Loosestrife"

I am indebted to the following gardeners whom I love and admire. Of
blessed memory: My father, who planted acres of vegetables to give away;
my mother, who loved red geraniums, bougainvillea and asparagus; John
Belsole, Henry Olsen, Esther Rome, Isabel Seimer, Robin Richman. Also,
the Rome family of gardeners, Jan Moss, Kathy Graven, Gina Murray,
Ev and Joan Shorey, Clay Taylor, Wini Smart, Renita Sheesley Banks,
Sally Schwager, Jolinda Osborne, Sharon Hulbert, Pamela Hill Nettleton,
Susan Allen Toth – and Donna Sonday, without whom I would have
no garden at all. Special gratitude to Jim Perlman for his open heart and
belief in my work and to Liz Tufte for the excellence of this book design.

for James C. Gertmenian,
gardener of spirit

Contents

V. Hideous with grief...

VI. What can be won...

VII. Beauty: cunning, bluff, superabundant...

VIII. For another try...

"The supernal vacuum is like a field in which are sown ten points of light. Just as each grain of seed grows according to its fertile power, so does each of these points. And just as seed cannot grow as long as it maintains its original form – growth coming only through decomposition – so these points could not become perfect configurations as long as they maintained their original form, but only from shattering."

~ Daniel C. Matt
The Essential Kabbalah

"So the flowers may be a balm or, if not a balm, some sort of gesture signifying the balm she would apply were it in her power to offer redress."

~ Paul Harding
Tinkers

First Shoots

How? In such a small case
does the bulb
pack all those petals and leaves?

෴

Of cold's cramped quarters
they've had enough!
Bulbs blow their tops and come out shooting.

෴

Curled up in the bulb
for the long, cold sleep, the leaves
dreamed these escaping blades.

෴

Green fingers poke through
blank, cold brown, testing:
safe enough yet for flowers?

෴

If I meditated a whole season
in a bulb-like cell,
would I too thrust up green?

I

If I had only one day...

Peepers

This was the sound at the beginning.
The quickening chant spelled over the deep
to call up substance, brooding over
the speechless waters until they rang.
Like the notes frost-bitten flesh would reach
tingling back to feeling, each warmed layer
of tissue jingling its little bell,
they rub the earth's bare, numb surface
with their constant, abrading carol
to bring up the green.
Swarming around the swamp's cauldron
they bewitch bulbs to toll their yellow clappers
and burst forsythia like stars from
the primal bang.

Loosestrife

Yes, all around Montgomery,
true to its name, in marshes
half-frozen and flooded in March
when I was through here, now
in mid-August, all that was bog
and dank weight has gone up
in red-purple flares.
They're showing us how:
Tell the sin that pits your insides
like gravel wheel-spun and spun
against metal; unhammer the spike
from the heart of what
you can't have or change,
let your wounds open like mouths and
bellow, bellow, and the strain unrolls.
Your flesh chills when you see it:
the color of something unburdened burning.

"Flowers That are Truly Orange are Relatively Few"

~ A Field Guide to Wildflowers

Along the road to town daylilies
lean out to catch me.
Don't you see, they would say
when they had me
in their stamens,
how orange we are?
Feel. Almost flesh.
Almost flame.

As I go they bob in my mind.
If *I* had only one day,
I'd want to burst as they do:
peeled out, with feelers,
bold as leaping cossacks
trumpeting over green –
starfires,
with petals soft
as the cheeks of a child.

Sonnet for February 23

Snowdrop beaks have pecked up through the cold crust
like chicks resting from the effort of chipping their shells.
Earlier light eases the effort of waking and later spells
me like kitchen help – a boost when whipping up custard
for the evening meal. Too, this increase releases song. Just
now a friend phoned. She'd heard the first titmouse swells.
Now we'll drill maples for the amniotic gush, our spiles
dripping diamonds we'll boil down to gold. And we must
brave the slush, this fuscous grit, to get to the clearance
sales. Only a rack of dark frocks left in a sea of turquoise, pinks
and yellows. Cat fur clogs the vacuum; commas of dog hair announcing
new clauses, cling to upholstery and clothes. I've glanced
at the nursery marquis: "Seeds" replace "Houseplants" and I think
of them, teams, huddled in packets, waiting for their chance to shout.

Prayer

You fill with an anguish.
It swells you. It strains
like a bud against its sepals.
you fear its power,
the explosion of its color.
You want to purse yourself,
repel its surge
and drive this dreadful sap
back into the ground,
but you let it burst,
allow the petals of your pain to fan out,
layer and array themselves
around your tender center.
The air is charged
with ultraviolet, and this
is what draws the Bee:
that all out opening up,
the quick of you disclosed.
She works you for all you're worth,
bagging your dust, drinking your blood,
until, drunk,
She rubs some of your male into your female,
doing the sex that brings a seed out of this death.
The rest she converts to viscid gold.

Trellis

Never built anything
before, but this year
couldn't let clematis
droop and break. I
procured the narrow
lumber, nails myself,
measured, pencilled
equal lengths, sawed
at the marks. Some
splintered, not quite
straight. Bent some
nails too, but it stands,
capable, at least, in
white paint. As it went
up, I thought of friends,
their arms and words
stretched out like rungs,
of spirit's resuscitating
puffs, the crisscross
structure on which my
shoots wind and pull
themselves, enabling me
now to build, to hold aloft
deep purple wheels.

Just Time

A day at last with no agenda
but to notice
how its stem bows,
as if in curtsy to a queen,
when the bee lands
in the geranium's cerulean cup.
How weighty is the bee
and how light
the leaves of its balm,
trembling with expectancy
at the merest current
as the hummer comes,
its back glistening with a green
of far more moment
than any tender,
drawn inextricably
to the flower's red blaze.
To be the object of such desire,
to be so wildly alive,
to let death whet the blade
of experience
and have one's essence be
to another
utterly essential,
for sips of it
to keep aloft
such scintillance.
Ah...

II

Sweet for its limit...

Sparklers

Late coming dark.
Stars burn through indigo.
Out on lawns children in nighties
filmy as nebulae hold before them
stars, like their own lives, on stems:
silver thornflowers, light slivers
dashing into oncoming night.
Their faces lit by the aura expand,
awe-stretched, charmed by
the quickness, the brightness.
They twirl them, making dark paths on the air.
Adults hang back in the doorways, knowing.
Collapsing mass, like novas, supernovas,
we expend ourselves,
hot, fleet, resplendent.
The course of our burning floats
black against blacker for moments,
tangled helixes dreaming,
against the acrid aftersmell of ash,
to prevail.

Redbuds Remembered

for RSB

Occasional visitor to the South,
I've only caught them once at
their peak, blue-pink veins
shooting through the peridot
mist veiling all other trees,
infusing the year, the viewer
with new, almost lavender blood.

This year I'm too early. Virginia's
woods are still bleak, still dun.
Their skinny trunks are camouflaged
among locusts and hophornbeams.

Yet the memory invigorates.
They flash up through thick,
stick-like shadows of thought,
upside down lightning,
volts of a pink
like unto nothing else that
jolts my slumbering wits
and gets me wondering if
this *imago* has more power
than the actual tree; if, when
so enshrined by the mind,
the real exceeds itself.

Already ~

in a flash, it seems,
the petals of the peony
have dropped
like so much magenta tissue,
tear-soaked, to the ground.
They, who just day
before last, splashed
the moving air with their brilliance,
causing passersby to gasp
not able to believe
color so wild, so hyper-toned.
Summer has just come!
How can the arc of light
already be turning down?
I don't want to see
the mess they make, florific
trash, crumpled, browning
leaving the stem, the bare
knob of the stigma bereft of blossom,
sentinel, lonely now,
through the seasons' round.
I don't want to be reminded,
as this month two friends,
my age, and like the year,
just past their prime,
have fallen, how fast –
no. NO – how fast it goes.

Leaving

I pull up the last tomato stalk and survey the yard:
a warp of quaking aspen weave with the Susquehanna.
Next door, Harold's apple tree amputated by
the weight of limbs so full of fruit.
Behind, the abandoned lumber yard once piled
with cement block hives and bare black
raspberry canes that volunteered sweet, soft
tangs against the roofs of our mouths.
The car is packed; the movers gone.
I click off the light switch in the living room.
It echoes.

Over the fence on the other side, a maple sapling
gives all its yellow leaves to a sudden bidding of wind.
Something, a larger world for my seeds to sail
and spin down to root, has called me beyond
this little town where casseroles appear on the stoop
when babies come or someone dies or for no reason
you can figure, and down at the Bake Shop
old men joke and grumble as donuts
Don Reithoffer rose at 3 to press out and fry
crumble sweet as life in their mouths.

All that's left is the friendship quilt
folded by the door. I finger the
embroidered signatures like Braille
and feel Linda lowered down so unready
and so young, Sharon no matter what, no matter
when pouring me a hot black welcome, Lola
in her schoolhouse by the corn field teaching me
to can August for January, and, on the pulpit,
Charles' snowdrops ringing in every Spring.
Good-bye brings the blood to our faces
as warp rends from weft and cords
of the Susquehanna ravel down, on down.

Revelation

Balmy, the air of a June night
rummages through new leaves
for something.
Something lost? Something
never found?
You're out in it, just standing
at the foot of the drive,
letting wind play softly over your flesh.
A tryst is imminent surely.
Your blood swells and crests,
breaking for shore. What shore?
A lover whose ministrations could
make your body belt out its song,
sending it like a wild flaming bird
into the night? No.
No love you can even imagine
could possibly answer the pounding
your heart delivers against time.
Yet, you're ready as the blown irises nearby,
your violet fallen away from the pink
you hold up tremulous, and
it comes to you with a pang
deep as space itself
that death
is the only thing
to solve your desire.
It is the sweet, consummate annihilation
that will free you finally into this wind,
into breath.

III

Mad flashes into the blue...

Fifteen Year Tribute

Buttocks, belly, the backs of my thighs,
parts I want to hide because
gauged against models, they've never
been firm enough or flat. Your strokes
though make them smooth and clean
as a leper kissed by a saint.
Intent on the goal, you couldn't always
linger in these places lavishing.
Nor could I trust
the quick of me to your hand
and expand like a stem
extending leaves, letting
you raise buds that burst,
many petalled, many
layers of petals.
It's taken years of pounding
on you till you heard me,
and you shaking me,
shaking me when I was
cold to your pain, but now
I rise from our bed, from
your loving, a blossom
lush as a tree peony,
deep pink,
to fill and
color in my name.

Dreamland Cafe

was the only place we could meet.
To get there, we didn't have to
leave our regular lives – just slip out
the door at the back of our minds.
Wind swept us down a street that
ended at the beach. We always knew
it was there but couldn't find it on
maps – a queer little place, perilously
close to the tideline; even neaps
wash it away, but it keeps reappearing.

There was a fire going. Old pews had
been cut down into seats, and on the
placemats, were wreaths of gamboling
cherubs and crows. He ordered a Molson;
I stuck to herb tea. He said he'd
tried to put me out of his mind, but
I'd kept coming back like a hungry cat
who can leap a fence or squeeze under
the gate. Thoughts of me rubbed up
against him and purred. What could he
do but feed? So there we were.

It wasn't like a real meeting.
Across the table our hands
went right through each other.
Our words orbited the forget-me-nots
between us, the candles, their
shimmying, turquoise flames.
What a nimbus they made!
In a way we were closer than when
our flesh had borders – passing in
and out of each other like breath,
but I missed the friction, the sensation.

When the food came – we had to
take what we were served: sole,
asparagus spears and confetti rice –
we savored every morsel.
For an after dinner
drink, they gave us lacrimosas with
twists of moonlight.
We toasted our demise
and paid the check by reaching
into the bottom of our hearts.
Back on the salver came mints with
a sharp, sweet taste we still
can't get off our tongues.

Bringing Them Back Out

You saw my flowers.
They'd been growing
by the side of the house.
Even I
wasn't fully aware of them.
Their colors caught your eye
from the road – palest pink
blushing to rouge, to rose.
You wanted a closer look.
They didn't see you coming.
The didn't have time to close up.
They were drowsing in the sun,
wind ruffling their
delicate, crinkly petals.
Before they opened their eyes,
they could feel you
looking down into their cups,
into their firm centers
girdled with stamen,
arrayed like garters on
Aphrodite's cestus with
its power to excite love.
You were tingling.
You were flushed.
You wanted to know them –
their names, their properties,
everything else.

I quivered.
The fur on their slender stems
stood up.
They had never yet been
beheld.
You adored them like
living icons, then
turned and continued your quest.

If you could come upon
such petals, such mantles,
there must be even greater
beauties further on.

They withered.
They dropped to the ground
and were swallowed up.
Once they had awakened,
had thriven under your gaze,
they couldn't go on alone.
But I hid in a pyx,
a small round altar receptacle
carved from mother of pearl,
the seeds of that consecrated moment.

I've been afraid until now
to bring them out.
What if they struggled back
into bloom and were ignored
as before, passed over.
How stupid and lonely I'd feel.
How exposed. How crushed.
So I've kept them all to myself.

I've warmed the mass of
tiny black periods for years
with secret attentions.
I've moistened them with tears.
But my time is running out.
Why not cast them abroad?
I want to see again
what will sprout –
if only for my own pleasure,
those translucent crinolines
reddening at the edges
with dawn.

Cain's Alternative

If you do well, will you not
be accepted? And if you do not
do well, sin is crouching at
your door; its desire is for you,
but you must master it.

Genesis 4:7

It's been twenty winters of wind
moaning through my stubbled fields.
Cold mornings, my teeth mashed grain,
a paste on my tongue.
Waiting,
the power of seeds building
for a chance to open ground again
and pour what I am into darkness,
to trust that
something will scream out
of its small, hard casing,
a singing vine.

All my beautiful produce
I gave Him: Look, look,
pomegranate, wheat, and olive.
The colors alone would woo Him.
Black, gold and, inside the fruit,
a trove of rubies.
I loved to look on them,
feel their flavors in my mouth.
But he turned and smiled on
goats, stroked their hides,
embraced my brother.
It was blood,
because they had blood,
or some such thing I was told,
my ears ringing, my face

falling like a shaken tower.
If it was blood He wanted,
I would give it to Him,
smear His precious one's blood
over my jilted fields.
As if I hadn't worked
my blood into that ground!
My fruit throbs with it.

Anger built like thunderheads.
I cocked the knife,
glinted my pain
over Abel's shoulder.
I wanted to tear the tending heart
that made God love him,
and He could never turn his face from me again.
My magic would spring up over the whole ground.
But I looked down into the loam,
dark, moist, calling me
home. I lowered my hand.
The ground had stayed me,
and Abel walked off unknowing.

I knelt down and cried into it,
as into a mother's lap.
"Why doesn't He like me?
I did the best I could."
But having Abel gone
would not help. Grief
would spoil my work for God.
My crops would stand before Him
like corpses. No matter how
deep I buried him, his stench
would drive me from my fields. And that
was the one thought impossible to bear,
to be cut off from working the ground.

So I kept at it.
The first year's harvest was rage,
fire vegetables: peppers,
white radish, tomatoes.
They rumbled, but we kept them down.
Some days favored laughter
from the pasture roared in my ears,
slowed my plow to a stop.
But somehow I heaved it ahead,
till finally my back was the blade
curling waves of soil
into welcoming furrows.

The earth gave under me
like a lover's flesh.
My sweat yielded
not only fruits – the peach,
with juices running from it
like a spring, the slender bean
to keep us going – but flowers:
bougainvillaea licking magenta
fire up the side of the house,
verbena's purple eyes.
No sounds mocked
me from the pasture, only wind
humming through my plant's leaves,
fluttering them like flags.

This morning I was out to hoe.
The melons shone,
their vines furling green
improvised flute tunes,
their fruit round, ripe, and yellow
in skins pulled over them like drums.
I looked up.
The sky's implacable blue had
broken into a smile.

I Really Want to Know

Given the absolute fact of death
why bother to paint an ancient Volvo
two shades of yellow: mustard, butter,
and drive it all over town with flair,
or grow a patch of dahlias
rampant with color, each petal
pointed as a rapier
or sing as if your soul were a seed
splitting open?
Why leave behind monuments,
testaments, towers of art
for those, like you, like me who too
will eventually have to leave?
To ease the bloody passage?
To distract from the end ahead?
And why love, why love
with everything you have,
which is only, as it turns out,
quickly witherable flesh,
especially when it's not returned
or spurned? Why send mad flashes
into the blue, into the dark?

in loving memory EW, EA, BW, WG, TH

In the Sierra

for JCG

Mountains sweep before us sheer
and expansive as death.
Seeing them still snowed in August,
heaved up above broad, coniferred skirts,
plays me high and deep,
an unstopped organ.

We're headed for the lake,
miles down this gutted
one lane road with dropoffs either side.
Lupines dust the way with pointed blues,
and here and there, scarlet penstemon
scatter blood drops.

But we do reach it, pack in, pitch our tent,
strike a fire at base of
this vermillion-cliffed valley
that yawns like an open crypt.
At dusk, wind catches light slices
in the water, masses of
white wings clamoring.

You prepare our freeze-dried food,
a chicken stew. Ashen crumbs
come to color. We hold
our coffee cups like prayers and
watch night flatten riffles,
the water waiting –
black silk for stars to pierce.

Inside the tent I'm keen
and shivering. Wind
through these Jeffrey pines with
red bark deep-grooved as graves
searches me.
Everything in this country
peals with silence.

Morning brings up a blue in the water,
wild iris blue, sharp enough
to slit the last sheath of my casing.
We slip out of our clothes and
go into it. It's cold,
so cold, but once our flesh accepts it,
then, on a blanket by the shore,
my loins give and give to you
as this lake gives over and over
into that stream,
and it wouldn't matter any more
if this were the end.

I Was Love (Rick '87)

Graffiti on the wall of a shelter along the Appalachian Trail

In this berth perched on a ridge
that seems a hinge between two worlds
it isn't clear whether stars fell like snow
to light the valley or the valley was
shaken like a blanket, its lights
flung up to relieve the dark.
Here one night the author of this
fantastic claim became their vessel.
Awe at this vast, luminary host
opened an inward bowl, where,
stirred by the wind, it
could pour into him and swirl,
clockwise and widdershins both. Oh!
The rooted, heady feeling from
that spinning! And with the
swelling of his wonder at it,
the speed of its wheeling grew.
All the little lights, the whirling
halo of scintillas merged into a fire.
He wept for he had been so cold,
and the moist heat burst the hard,
dry casing of his heart into a bloom
so red and fresh and fragrant,
the ground would open of itself
to receive the seed meteors freed
and floating from its center.
He turned to the woman beside him
with whom he shared the trail
and found that at last all
barriers between them
had been felled.
He infused her with himself

and drove her blood beyond its channels
teeming over her edges in
cataracts of singing light.
And tonight at this intersection where
heaven turns to earth and earth to heaven,
when I traced these bold blue letters,
rivers of stars flowed into me through my fingers
and I was love too.

IV

That they will still be here...

Photographing the Lady's Slipper

for PP

It was the way she went about it,
swift through the woods, bending low,
moving from one to the other, avid
to catch them now, late May, in full flower.
They'd thinned, she said, since
she came here as a child. She crouched
(at our age, no small trick), adjusted the aperture,
zoomed in, focused on the proud
magenta bulge, the striated pouch,
the spathe curled over, hood-like, crimson,
the leaves and side petals extended
lissome as arms of the ballerina she once was.
At the time, I wondered at her urgency.
Why, with all else that pressed on her – and there
was much – did this seem
the most important thing in the world?
There was no way of knowing then, but since,
the land's been gouged, and where they once were
are condos now.
Because of people with passions like hers
our children's children will have the images, at least.
Whatever will they make of what once was wild?

The Greenway

for Mary Lou & Warren Loud

We will have twelve lanes
running through
the heart of our city. How else
will we get anywhere?
But then we grasp back at green,
our need for it and flowers
as the filament of a dream
we want desperately to recapture.
We trim the lanes with gardens,
with grasses we won't let
get out of hand like the native ones,
taller than we are, we eradicated
to inhabit this freezing prairie Eden
perched on the bluffs of our greatest river,
an open wound, riving our nation in half.

We cram a cultivated circle
with every flora we can grab
as if to offer a bouquet of apology
to the earth, to make amends
to what we've done to the wild.
Strips of green wind alongside concrete
paths, bandages, patches of green gauze
trying to soften and bind all the hardness.
We commission a fanciful wooden bridge
to connect the gardens across the lanes,
decorate its length with lines of poetry
to transcend the rush. Together
we walk this way we've made
as the Israelites sang songs of Zion
in exile, congratulating ourselves.
There! we say, *We've made a place*
in our habitat for nature, but we can't
hear each other over the roar.

Hoh Rainforest, Olympic Peninsula

for Emily

We have almost ruined the earth,
say I, who ate my lunch from a Styrofoam bowl
and threw away a big plastic bag
at the "last chance" café on the Park border.

This is the land of clouds.
They swim over us like a pod of ethereal whales,
underbellies pregnant with rain or
extend long tendrils lingering on the mountainside
as on shoulders of a beloved, reluctant to leave.
That line of jagged, snow-stroked peaks
matches the print-out my cardio tape
as I look on them would read.
Streams quiver with the almost incessant beating.

We can still go to corners like this
where so much rain
has cleaned, at last,
to a shining, the air,
where trees are left to rise,
no axes raised to them,
as high as they can,
their branches shaggy
in sleeves of soft mosses,
the mosses plumed with ferns.
Here they're allowed
to go punky, to fall on cushions
laid down lush,
brocaded by their forbears,
        green upon green,
to die and decay into food
for all who spring up ever after.

No more species lists, the rangers say,
to keep the hundreds of inventive names
for lichens, liverworts: *pencil script,*
devil's matchsticks, fairy barf.
Copying costs too much during war.
I would rather forego the gas it takes
to get here, certainly the blood spilt
to control its source, and never see
these queenly colonnades
dripping like goddesses emerging
over eons from primeval waters
just to know they are here,
that they will still be here....

Hamburger

I'm talking patties you shape yourself,
thick, out of meat red with innocent blood,
barbecued in 90 degree heat till juices
run off them like eroding rain, till
globules of fat form like river-
clogging silt and they smell
heady as a birthright, till they're
black as acres slashed
and burned for pasture.
I'm saying these burgers are
slathered with whatever you want –
ketchup, piccalilli, mayo. Lay it on.
This is the American icon.
The burnt offering that *is* God.
Slap it on a bun,
sink your teeth in,
and bite off a chunk of jungle
five times the size of Manhattan –
what gets cleared every day for
the beef we're eating to graze on.

Clear-winged butterflies, lemurs, pangolins.
Scads of bromiliads, orchids, weaver ants.
Trees: the ceiba, the chanta, the sealing wax palm.
Basilisks, who water walk, poison arrow frogs.
Click beetles with bioluminescent dots.
Geckos, gibbons, gurania. Pit vipers, pythons.
Silk moths, who startle their predators with
eye-like spots. Lianas, wolf spiders, sugar gliders.
Lorikeets, oropendulas, browneas,
their huge scarlet explosions.
Legions. Legions. Legions. – all
chopped meat, $1.59 a pound.
And when they're gone,
feast on your own breath.
Taste the cost.

Haleakala

Up through a crown of clouds that weeps over it,
arraying it with rainbows,
past silver swords raising their blades
                 against us,
on a road that goes higher,
             faster than any in the world,
we gain this peak
hauled up from the depths by a god and
built this high by sheet after sheet of liquid fire.
Not what we'd hoped, the crater is
      not a lush cavity, a color spectacle.
It is Pele's mouth
      sealed over, silenced
         just after Captain Cook –
an earth sore, pocked with cinder cones,
a lesion, scabbed,
gagged anger that bloomed rock "bombs"
         and kupaoa, torch flowers
ablaze with gold found nowhere else.
           Nowhere else
but on these slopes
         does the scarlet *i'iwi* bird
         sip with its arced bill
from the sweet red tufts of the *'ohi'a lehua*,
           traces
      of the divine passion that gave rise to
           this special world.
And that's why we have to see it, want to
celebrate like natives
        with arms and hips that move
      like waves and wind and clouds.
So we come, bringing our story of the serpent,
   germs,
     and we are welcomed –
      Aloha, beloved, fellow being.

We bring hotels
    cropping up like growths
    too many, too fast along the shore
        craning for the view –
   Molokai,
    its dark, wimpled mass rising
from the turquoise water like a great ship.
  When it sails each night into the dark,
     Pele's dreams
    rattle our condo skylights
     flip the knockers on our doors.
A flow of words rumbles up from her core
that would wipe this island clean again,
but when we get up to check
    nothing but a trade wind,
    tying song around the building,
    answers.

Bravo

Bravo! I said to the mountain,
Colorado mountain,
you have made yourself
too high and steep,
your slopes too forbiddingly angled
for humans even to climb
let alone develop and settle on.

Hold on! Last blades of tall grass
holdouts in hills
too flinty to plow.
Way over our heads,
hold high, your blue plumed crowns.

You go, walruses!
Float away on ice floes
in currents too treacherous
for hunters or photographers.
Rub the recovering numbers
of your calves with your whiskered muzzles
and show *us* your tusks.

Hurrah! you pale,
yellow-winged moths,
camouflaged by smog,
under cover of one enemy,
giving others the slip.
enlist our iniquities
to keep flittering.

Up with you hummers!
Flower slurpers, nectar burners.
Zip, zap, dazzle, flash.
You extend your range,
expand your palate, poking

blooms to accommodate your proboscis
with brains, relative to body size
bigger than ours,
streak, jewel green, right by us.

High microscopic five, you mites!
crawling through our follicles,
gorging our dermal detritus,
and we, totally oblivious.

Viva! Live even longer, coastal redwoods.
Tallest trees, tallest living beings
in the world, your beauty,
venerable elders,
deep-grooved, your delicate,
fog-sipping needles
saved at least some of you
and stopped our axes cold.

Weeds

console me even as I try to
rout them from this skirt of
shrubs. In the week since
I last had at them with
garden-gloved hands and a
claw, there are a lot more,
and they're bigger than before
poking up through inches of
mini-chips I sweated spreading
that were supposed to hold them
down for the sake of rhodies,
hollies, lilies, azaleas. These
are prized by the civilized
more than spurge and knavel,
more than cheat and pokeweed,
smartweed, toadflax, and hoary
vervain, which are impertinent,
insidious and virulent. Of course,
I too want a nice neat yard,
so out they go, piles and
piles of them dumped from the
wheelbarrow into the back lot
where they belong. Our plots
are blotting out so much wild.
Yet, in a matter of weeks
crabgrass growing unchecked
between the flagstones
almost swallows them. Checking
can be a full-time job; I can't
keep up with the likes of nimblewill –
so I bow to its greater power
and relax in the thought that
when we're all gone, the weeds
I'm damning now will green over

all we've done. Healall
will close the scars we've cut
with roads and parking lots,
and maybe in several years a vine
like bindweed could climb the
Empire State, the Sears Tower
and with its pink, funnel-like
flowers pull them down
into the Mother's bosom.

Georgetown Walkabout

with Joan & Ev Shorey

Threatened by disease and age
how much longer will we be able,
as we are today,
to take the afternoon,
glee leaping from our throats
at minute snowdrop hankies
popped down by your front stoop
and winter's end wind rubbing against us –
to whet or mark itself?

We imitate to tease it, a nattering crow.
Earlier, through your kitchen window,
morning sun cast shadows of cedars
over our breakfast dishes,
bowing and shaking.
You have been taken for my parents.
More's the wonder, we are friends.

Dumbarton Oaks, the garden is barred.
Ice still too thick on the flagstones.
But at Tudor Place, for more
than two centuries owned
by kin of our country's mother,
we can smell in the acrid box
the accretion of time,
and the winterberry has kept
its beady red faith through every
assailment of cold.

Together we worry, what can we do
to prevent our nation's lifeline
from being broken?
Yesterday, at the Holocaust Museum
we clutched each other and wept.

On the way back we bend to pick up
rosette cones, attracted by their pattern
of overlapping scales – inside each one
after all, a seed for starting over.

We'll set them on a shelf
with other objects we collect
important to our souls:
Prattware, lusterware, ceramic bowls.
What will they tell those we leave
about who we were?

On our return, at the back door,
the winter jasmine pours
into the falling dark, a cascade
of small yellow stars.

V

Hideous with grief...

Rabbit's Foot Clover

It's not quite luck I feel, coming upon,
hard by the pavement, angling up
out of gravel, their luminous,
silvery, pink-tinged fur,
their leaflets at the stem joints
in modest, charm-time threes
but more – comfort, like a softness
had just brushed my hard-pressed cheek.
They're plusher than Q-tips, but suggest
the swabbing of burns or sponges
wetted on sticks to ease for the dying
their thirst. No luck anyway can ever
ultimately take the "t" out of "stave."
Think of the hare's poor bloody – leg.

To Touch the Wound

"Rub this neck incision twice a day with cream,"
the surgeon said, "two full minutes each time."
I weaken and flinch, touching the welted seam

that opened like a mouth to speak my blood, a wine
fermented under skin and poured to purge my throat
of a growth, a mass of tears wound up like twine,

a string of trials and draughts that made me choke.
It could not be untangled – I couldn't cry – so it was cut.
They say if you massage a scar, stroke

it diligently for months, the tissue smooths out
and the line that drew death close almost disappears.
Yet, if I had dared to try and soothe that knot,

not swallowed it away, but put my fingers
in the strands and coaxed them loose, sought
fervently to ease the strain and persevered

as if along a stem to find the roots, and saw
them dangling Gorgon's hair, the effort that it took
might have strengthened me, struck stony by that awful

down-turned head hideous with grief, to look and look
until it resolved into the mother that I missed.
Then sorrow might have flowered in a gorgeous bush
and they'd not have had to slit my throat for this.

Back From the Funeral of a Twelve-Year-Old

Stupid target practice accident.
My daughter's classmate,
no one very close, but death
has a way of tracing
all our crooked tributaries
to the same source.
It's rainy and cold.
My body feels leaden,
skin quick to
the chafing of these clothes.
Think of the mother,
whose shot it was,
of the ghastly fact
dawning on her every morning,
streaking the sky with his blood.
Raindrops are streaming down
all the windows of this town.
The only good I can see
is sixth grade girls and boys
gingerly stroking
each other's arms,
the divorced parents' hug,
the flood of flowers,
and my daughter, who'd usually
scorn it in front of friends,
wanting my hand,
turning her dear, stricken
face up to me.

Gettysburg Monuments

A weird crop of stone and bronze
springs up among ribbons of hops and corn
near farmhouses, barns, the town, the campus:
Pillars, monoliths, some chiseled
with names of states or the fallen,
topped with balls, stars, crosses, laurel, clover,
figures of men and their horses, soldiers,
winged goddesses, guns.
Fertilized by 51,000, in just three days all
become corpses – close to the whole
American toll in Vietnam –
these huge petrified blood flowers,
perpetual blooms to how hard,
how desired is Union,
cannot so easily be cut down,
or harvested.

Cherry Blossoms

after Basho & Issa

for PBI

White tears scatter the sky
around the Basin where blossoms spread,
but the time of flowering soon goes by

in Washington. We came there to cry
"Stop B-52's!" raining their dread
white tears that splatter the sky

over children too dumbstruck to ask why
their homes burned, their parents bled.
Their time of flowering too soon went by.

Holy Week, when with a jailed fast we tried
rolling away stones from those tombs, we shed
white tears that spattered the sky.

After, you plucked a branch, thrust it in my
hands and said, "This is our soul's bread."
But our time of flowering soon goes by,

and pressed between Psalms, those petals dry,
unlike my eyes and the Psalmist's. We've fed
on white tears battering the sky
for our time of flowering so soon gone by.

Bulbs

I overdid it this year,
probably a response, unconscious,
to the terrors and bombs, the plagues,
the devastated faces of the bereft.
I bought more bulbs than I could afford,
than I had room for, than I could plant
without blisters and soreness
from driving them down into dirt.
I was overcome by the promise
of their colors: by gradations
of pink from deep to pale and back
again through "peerless" to warm-blooded
red, by striations of peach and lavender,
whites purfled with mauve,
ruffles and apricot horns,
by the thought of their cheek-soft flesh,
the bounce back they could portend.
I got drawn in. It took my mind off
the sweater found at ground zero
with only a sliver of bone in its arm.
As I put them in, smooth tulips,
ragged daffs, I thought, These, at last
are big enough tears, big as I feel,
bigger than my eyes can form.
Let me plant this grief
and let it explode like surrogate
landmines at someone's feet
into *flowers*, enough
to cancel some of the harm.

Parkville

Fill the earth and subdue it.
Genesis 1:28

Last night I dreamed the sleepy river village
I began in had changed into an upscale suburb.
The single pump on the corner
with its winged horse had
been replaced by a Sheraton with
views we never knew we had before
of Spring willows letting their golden hair
down over the eddying flow.
Though it was marred even then with
eyesores: billboards and
car hulks rusting in our ravines.

Why could we never see it before?
Why did it need framing?

The drug store, now the Video Hut,
was once the only place to go
when temperatures rose over 100,
its slow, soundless overhead fan
and fountain with the marble counter
an 8-year-old could cool her cheek on
waiting for Mr. Long to squeeze
lime juice into a tall, fluted glass.

When did we start to choose the can
on the screen over the glass in our hands?

Fast food out on Rt. 34 did away with
biscuits and gravy with watermelon pickle
and closed Chet's Shopwell downtown where
you could learn more buying groceries than
reading *The Current.* While the butcher
wrapped your ground chuck you could
wonder aloud with Genevieve Weir where
Murt Henry went every afternoon in his pickup
and hope her concern about Murt would keep her
from counting how many times a week
you'd leave RiversEdge Liquors with a gallon.

How close is too close, but not close enough?
How far away is love?

"If we don't have it, you don't need it" –
Stone's Department Store and Hardware
across the street. Anything from garters
and seed to lugnuts, rick-rack,
cookie sheets and shoes, but not
the Finnish glass and haute couture
magazines made you yearn for
that those chic new boutiques carry now.
They brought down Stone's extra-high
hammered tin ceilings, but you still can't get
cappucino or sushi in this town.

Why do we have to have what we want?
Why don't we want what we have?

And they've paved the River Road
we used to bounce home on in our
mustard-gold '53 Chevy. Along the way,
bottomland generations of Oberhelmans
sweated corn out of, driving Sioux from
the ground they called Grandmother – ground
on whom every step taken was a prayer –

is being developed: raised ranches and condos.
Backhoes bite deeper each day into space
whose blank page eggs us to mark it,
edging out warblers and bloodroot.

Once all the land is used up, what
will we write our stories on?

Most farmers have sold out, broken
by taxes and equipment costs. They
moved to the city where the only rows
are of houses or screens they say don't
satisfy like furrows, but they've had
their first vacation ever – to Disneyworld.
The houses are still there, weekend retreats
for urban professionals, a few cows left
as momentos still bawling in the corral.

What is progress? Does wildness beg to be tamed or
is taming a stab at stemming its threat to our power?

Nothing we could do stopped tornados or
drought, the grasshoppers who ate everything
one year but the peach pits.
We'd go down to the river for answers,
just watch it go and go like time
and dream the impossible: our stones
skipping all the way across.
Hands that made monuments in that mud
are speckled on their backs with brown snow
recalling larger spots on the toil-worn hands
of my grandmother, who'd shell peas
all afternoon and, though she was beat by
evening, canned them – green
to keep us all the way through winter.

What is the work that rewards? What is
the reward? What are we meant to do?

Nothing she did ever made money.
She tended the roses no one else would
fuss with. Present owners have turned them out
for junipers and pine bark mulch.
Bushes out front spanning the whole length
of the house ran the gamut from black-red
to bluish pink, to flame to lemon to snow.
she hummed, "I Love You Truly, Truly Dear"
and other pre-war favorites. Her touch,
producing mostly unbitten, mould-free leaves
and petals that unfolded slowly as a day,
a life, a story, a star, could not, however,
stop my brother's tantrums.
Locusts screamed and copperheads
sunned themselves on the awning's green,
or waited, camouflaged, on a stone step.

Was there ever a time before ruination?
Can memory take us there, can dreams?
Or are dreams no longer a recourse?
Can they form no Elysian vision, only
portray actions that have already been taken
by characters bearing our names?
What is the end of our dreams?

VI

What can be won…

Dry Creek Bed

Four Springs

I go down this gorge as I have before –
spent and sear, hoping God
is warbling over the stones.
I need a song to salve
the gulch of this wound.
I want to descend into the damp shade
and bloom on the banks like
roseroot. Wind rasps in the brush.
I wobble along the precipice
and skid on rubble.
Stellar's jays screech
from the blistered red
branches of the madrones,
while in the gourd my soul forms,
silence rattles.
I come to the stones, dry,
dull, unshining.
I could hurl them
to hurt it
against the sky.
Let its tears course
silken over me till
I slicken and croon,
till I emerge from the groin of
these sun-golded mountains,
new, renewed, my depths
exulting like a torrent.

Freedom

It's you, not characters
in novel or movie,
who can't escape that country,
the one with heavily guarded borders
and orders to kill on sight
anyone in your kind of flower.
No wonder your heart beats faster
when you see those others
tear down the rain-streaked
street on the screen
and flatten themselves
against a building in shadow.
Their love doesn't stand a chance
in this place and neither
does yours, though
it's something you can't help
like skin color or
the religion of your ancestors.
Yours is the odd, unruly plant
that clashes with their program
and they can't breathe
until they weed you out –
a threat, your color simply
disclosing itself.
Until now you've kept it
under cover, a rural greenhouse,
sheltered under a wave of
brambles, but it's
snapped the panes of those confines
with tongues the tone of
blood mingled with fire
which now can be
seen from the road.
So you run, holding
the blossom between you
like a torch, its

petals raining a
stinging benediction on
those along the route.
This, at least, is
glorious, this
pure searing,
this rush to the wall
you'll never clear
without tearing yourselves
to ribbons.

Baker's Cafe

A corner table,
old oak, grain
like a mother's wrinkled face.
A vase on it in winter.
Sprigs of larkspur,
white roses – petals
edged in red, pink
carnations: for a moment
something clear,
something vivid.
Extravagant though,
a stolen indulgence
to be fed, to be
asked what one would like
by a bright, lively
young woman in overalls
who looks kindly
into one's eyes
through fallen strands.
How to know?
Needs of others
always ahead.
How about…
Salad: a cloud of sprouts,
a bed of shredded carrots
on anointed greens.
Soup: a suspension of the Garden.
And bread warm, plump and
satisfying as the breast.
The juice today?
Lingonberry.
Dense purple elixir
for surviving
long darkness,
severe cold.
Laughter and chatter from

the open kitchen.
They seem to enjoy cooking.
It doesn't appear
to exhaust them.
All around the lulling
hubbub of garbled
conversation, children
shushing in and out of snowsuits.
An occasional snort or babycry,
otherwise, riverrun.
Let it carry the burdens off.
Dessert? Why not?
What from the display case?
Buttercake? Shortbread?
Chocolate frosted with
confetti sprinkles?
Just one large, dark
crackle-top ginger snap,
chewy and crisp
with tea – herbal.
Over it all on the walls, art.
Icon of the cup just drunk
and one feels in finger pads
the pressure of the handle.
Payment and tip accepted
with grace, smiles and
a friendly query about
the book in hand
there will never be
time to finish.
It's just a wish.
Through the glass door:
across the street
the iron beams
and grafittied concrete
of the station.
Wistful backglance.
Here, one cannot stay.

Solomon Visits the Queen of Sheba

Unquiet on his throne, as if
stirred within by flicks of
a serpent's winding length,
Solomon paces and broods – a mood
even lions, golden effigies
guarding his ascent to the ivory chair,
cannot whip away with their tails.
Outside, among the flowering
figs and pomegranate,
turtledoves coo
to a descant of hissing locusts.
The glory of the Temple has soured.
He feels smothered by cherub's wings,
by Yahweh's cloud in the Debir,
by so many holy ordinances.
Even his hundred, hundred wives
cannot give him succor.

The only boon is Sheba, beckoning
night after night in dreams,
turning in his waking mind like
a ruby refracting light from
its wine-dark core – Sheba,
Arabian monarch who plumbed him
with questions and went deeper,
confounding him with proverbs of her own:
The fool is wiser than the sage.
Abandon precepts, follow the moment's scent.
Only the naked are clothed in glory.
It takes both warp and weft to make cloth.
Tend the child like a rose and
let its nature unfold like a flower.

Her words swirled counter to
his learning, his teaching.
A whirlpool to pull him down and
drown him? Or was she merely

tugging, motioning him into a cave,
a deep dark whose floor is
shadowed with dancing?
At his pinnacle,
sated and wasting,
Solomon cries out.
The time has come to
go down to her.

Telling no one,
he leaves at night by chariot,
taking only the barest retinue.
Desert air, cool against his face
as death, keens in his ears.
Fixed on Orion's sword,
he heads south into
her enveloping essence,
fragrant in his mind as myrrh.
When the sun rises on his caravan,
it burns like Yahweh's anger.

He approaches her tents.
Joy and fear course through him,
joining in a single torrent.
He has never needed anyone before.
What will he gain from this mad venture?
No anointed king of Yahweh's
should bend his knee to
the priestess of a female god;
yet, that is what he wishes,
to kneel before her and ask
how he can feel the beat of his blood
again and taste the comfort of apples.

She is at her loom, taming a
riot of deep blues and reds
into a rayed medallion.
Children and women surround her.
Some pound grain in mortars,
others mend. Others still
play a game on the floor with pebbles

or dance to a tune fluted through reeds.
In a corner, men scrape frankincense from
bark, white as chunks of the moon,
Burning in a small brazier,
its sweet scent mingles with that of
camel milk cheese hanging from the crosspost.

My dear Solomon! she exclaims.
How wonderful to see you.
She is indeed beautiful, her eyes
darker, more lustrous than the lapis
she wears against her skin's gold.
Come join us. We've just discovered
what superb pictures we can make from
the wet, wilted petals of irises.
See. Isn't it marvelous?
They're a gift from these heavy spring rains.
Lovely, aren't they?
Yes, Solomon thinks,
lavender standards, deep purple falls
like brides disrobing for their husbands.
Why don't you try it? Sheba urges.
Stunned, he takes a petal
and moves it dumbly across papyrus.
His smudges reproduce the upraised
and down-turned petals of the flower.

I was afraid I would interrupt
your affairs of state, he says.
*But these **are** the state's affairs,*
she laughs. Why what do you mean?
This is what you do all day?
Yes, she smiles, *we've found that*
if we spend the better part of our time
this way, it lightens our duller tasks
and we get along so much better.
And where is your throne? Solomon asks.

I don't need one, Sheba replies.
We take turns washing, cooking,
lawmaking, trading. This six-year-old
is my consort now. He's shown us
the insect life of the desert,
the beetle-who-carries-the-night-on-its-back,
its white spots bright as stars
against its black – a whole
universe shining up at us from a particle.

He wonders how she gets anything
done like this. How are her
accounts kept, her people ruled?
And, since building has been
the sole aim of his kingship,
he wants to know why
she still lives in tents.
Doesn't she want something more
permanent, a monument, a home?
Your temple is magnificent, she grants,
but building saps delight.
Permanence is a mirage.
Our tents keep us from deluding ourselves.
All we have is this moment, this fruit,
to suck the sweetness from it while we can.
She slips a date between his lips.

Solomon retires to the tent she's
provided for him. What should he do now?
He can't live as she does,
in such disarray, so transient.
He can't go back to things
the way they are at home.
When he is near her,
his dry interior floods,
and his ground flowers
with lavender clouds like those he saw
hovering over the sand on his way here.
He sleeps.
Then, out of breath and sweating,
he wakes to his own screams.

In a dream his sons pursue him –
a pack of jackals.
He dresses quickly.
He must get back. His empty throne
has brought on Yahweh's rage.
Don't forget this, Sheba says,
presenting him with the image
he'd drawn the day before.
He accepts it.
They part with a kiss.

Going back, he is filled with
an unaccustomed peace,
as if his parched soul were
fanned by bending palms.
His chariots seem to float over the desert,
the way lit by brilliant flowers
she called, our desert candles.

Nearing Jerusalem, the Fountain Gàte,
Solomon spots Benaiah,
commander of his army with
a band of soldiers and Jereboam, his son.
His blood runs cold as Gihon's Spring.
He meets them. Benaiah speaks,
You once commanded me to kill
the enemies of Yahweh.
Now you yourself have turned from
the God of your fathers
and must accept the penalty.
His sword goes through Solomon's heart.
As his blood flows out,
he sees inside the cedar panels
of the ark's tabernacle
an iris lifting its plumed chamber
between tablets of the covenant,
and he drops, drops into the flower
bathed in its soft yellow light,
stroked by the rosy streaks of its interior.

What Can Be Won

It is enough this morning
that chicory blinks
its vault blue lashes
at the roadside
on spindles tentative
as foal's legs.

Some pain, some spading
horror: news from El Salvador –
men's heads shoved
in their slaughtered lover's
wombs and knowing you've
turned from your own crying child
shovels through thick skins
to a shutter and the film
silver enough to take
those cerulean tatters,
printed absolutions
as you go by.

Amaryllis

Spears of green stab
from the scruffy lump.
Were they crouched
in the bulb all along?
A mighty upthrust –
progress you can almost watch.
The tip cracks, beak-like
disclosing packed in bloom.
Little nestlings of bud
poke through, scramble out,
unseal, steal forth, red-flapped,
flares blaring at the window
like compass-pointed horn honks
for the cold to *move,* move ***off***!
Or is this the season's celebrant,
fanfare for the common sifting
of crystals, gritted drifts,
icy sidewalks? Maybe
sirens, not of warning –
earthquakes, tornados, air raids
wailing red at a pole top –
but protest for the victims'
conditions: wounded, ravenous,
encamped, dis-homed,
a blast, many-tongued
of their outsized anguish,
the enormity of it fully exposed.
How can we say something this
wanton is beautiful?
But doesn't beauty, more than
anything, force the doors
of the guarded heart open
to plunder the contents
and leave it bereft of defense
against affliction – others'
or our own? This outcry color

is stem-topplingly loud,
but scarcely enough to tumble
down walls to the promise:
flourishment for all.
Look, another stunner
is pushing up from the roots
to raise the alarming
standard of love.

Though

a wave of fire is poised over this house,
its habits of meals and sleep,
quarrels and loving, over this town
humming with traffic and trade, over
the world shot spinning into infinity;
though other threats make inroads
by the hour, sudden as a snake
gulping frogs' eggs, gradual
as lichen engulfing a trunk
to the hyacinth macaw,
the small whorled pogonia;
though we drive each other into cells
with words sharpened against
the stone of our fear and we are
alone in our skin and no one will know
what our eyes see last, still,
in this soft rain, green
has sprung from winter's hold,
wind strums water
caught in pits of pavement,
and your eyes have found the way
to the slope where my crocuses
lift their purple cups
to your lips.

VII

Beauty: cunning, bluff, superabundant…

Driving Through March Snow

White javelins aimed straight at me
is how I'd usually see these streaks
whose coming would shake my bones and
pump my life's blood up to shield me.
Not now, before a full flowering
with only snowdrops and a few crocus
to show from a whole repertory!
But tonight a curious peace
rises like sap up my trunk and
spreads all the way to my tips.
I'm taking two roads,
one superimposed on the other
like a double-exposed movie.
Going down Rt. 302, I speed through
stars that open out like petals of
a gloriosa daisy. I stream deep
into its black center, down the
dark hall of the seed, into
the split-open hull holding me
all the way home
to infinity.

Daffodil Valley

for Holly Blumner

In this gash of land
running rivulets cut,
in March, the month
of almost losing hope,
a gush of yellow wells up,
the color of health,
lush trumpets bellowing:
where there has been hurt,
it can be especially fertile.
In the crook of Earth's
elbow, a cradling
for the first heads up
from the dark below.

Please

Freckled, bespeckled world
peeping with green new leaves,
sprung with bud clusters yellow as gosling fuzz
that flood the cocoa brown undertrees
casting shadow-puffs we stroll beneath,
spirit-touched, doldrums buffed to sateen,
your catkins dangling hypnotically
sway in the arms of the breeze;
petaled pink pools soothe
the crabapple's feet, and bushes
break into high-pitched colorific glee.
Indulging in lilac's perfume, sweet drug,
in favors lolled blowsy over ice-released creeks,
in lily-of-the-valley tinkling star-white the dusk,
in irises' purple eruptions, gold shot,
even pollen powdering a junker's cheeks –
the whoosh, the tweetering, the buzz, the rush –
we split our capacity's seams and beauty
cunning, bluff, superabundant, overcomes us;
Spring, please! How will we ever
be able this earth to leave?

Peonies

for Susan Allen Toth

She's set them out in four vases
along her table's center, cuttings
from the numberless strains of them
she's nursed into splendiferous flower,
all stops of pink pulled out,
color of bliss, color of comfort –
muted to bravura: Lullaby Coos,
Kinkaku, Duchess de Nemours, Do Tell,
Torch Song, Hit Parade, Raspberries –
Sundae and Rhumba, Banner Bright,
Luxor, Cloud Cap, Minuet, Immaculee,
Splendida, Prairie Afire, and the one named T.,
after the dear dead friend who gave it to her,
nestled next to Friendship, Requiem.

Caring for her ailing husband, the moment
by moment travail of it depleting her: brushing
and flossing his teeth; making sure he actually
eats the luscious fish stew she's somehow
conjured; guiding him gently down steps
to the car now only *she* can drive; keeping
straight several times daily medications,
multiple, multicolored; securing non-disturbing
entertainments; arranging and taking him to
doctor's visits – a plethora, etc., ***etc.***, – in the wake
of this, with all the old religions now warring for dominance
and emptied of their power, we take in these blooms,
their full, flush, rain-dimpled faces, with *dazzlement*,
the collective she's invented for them together.

We're hushed but for wordless utterings of awe
and pleasure – the gush of their immanence,
their tender bristling staminodes like so many
healing fingers reaching for us. Our weary
barricades give way, for I too – don't we
all? – have burdens too heavy to shoulder.
Our membranes become permeable. In this space
she's made plush, made *church* by placing them here,
there is a sudden influx of nourishment, an assist given.
We could bury our tear- streaked cheeks
in their softness, ample with petal tissues to mop
and absorb into beauty our fears. *Now **that***, she says,
pointing at the lush, booming bombshells
of blossom, ***that***, she says, *is God.*

Lilacs

First, their limbs deliver valentines
of softest green, then,
tossing in May gusts like dancers
who have given up, given up
to the dance,
the bush is rapture animate.
Branches reach antlers
that at their tips
offer tiny damson nutmeats.
There is joyance in their shape,
the air of carnivals and treats:
fool's caps, miters,
lavender sugar spun on funnels,
a clutch of juggling pins
flourished before the feat, whirls
of amethyst tulle – hives,
the petals like insect wings
swarmed to create a fragrance
sweet as Spring's *parfum*:
Head Over Heels.

Hydrangea Blue

You can't believe a blue this bright, this
high-powered, but want to, need to.
It smacks of the more, the better
you hope to God will be beyond
what's visible, what's tangible, such as
the checking clapboard this bush is set against
or the black top cracking next to the soil
its roots are sunk in.
It's the same unworldly hue we take
to mosaic the vaults of basilica domes,
facsimile empyreans –
invariably chosen for the virgin's mantle.
Long looks at it inoculate pilgrims against
the rusty bloods, the sallows, smokes and
duns of the grind outside the sanctum, and
it matches the color hearts turn when,
in prayer, they break out of themselves.
It intimates Providence can be near
and will bloom for you,
but only in acid ground; otherwise,
it pales to greenish yellow.
So it's not other, not made up, but
here, natural, right at your
back door, the kitchen door
next to the recycling bin,
umbels, exploded globes, of
a higher intensity blue
than any heaven you can imagine.

Sniffing

Watching her black, moist nostrils
twitch and flare, testing the air as
a bather would dip a toe in water,
I've often wondered how it would be
for smell to be the keenest sense
and such a keen sense; for whiffs
of fresh-cut grass to send you into
delirium, so you wriggle on your
back in it till you're spent and drowsy.
To follow the lush, musky trails of
woodchuck, moles, squirrels and cats
that make the lawn an invisible
buzzing matrix of scents and to be
propelled, at times, to cannon velocity.
The chase – what a thrill to be so whetted!
And how cathartic for the stench of enemy
to be so foul you break into a barking fury!
What is it the UPS man reeks of anyway?
More subtly, to be able to pick up a
drift on guests you can't otherwise admit
you're wary of, as if they were dowsed in
the fooling English Leather of a gigolo,
and to snap instinctively. I applaud such
pluck – and such capacity for ecstasy.
The exotic attar exuding from the backsides
of prospective mates must be redolent as if
with balsam or clove. And whenever we
come home, she inhales us like the blanketing
bouquet of baking bread, or – barbecuing
steak, the one scent dearer to her than we.
I've seen her sit by the grill, her snout
upraised, sniffing decorously as if doing
homage to a great power, God's glory
having distilled itself into the incense of
that sizzling meat. Right now, at an open

window, paws on the sill, she's assessing
the aroma of rain. Her half-closed lids
and sighs say it must be teeming with lilies.
I'm jealous. Yet most of all, though I
yank on the choke chain whenever she strains
toward it, I marvel at her passion for
excrement. She relishes garbage too,
the compost heap, all rotting things.
I wonder what it would be to perceive
the fragrance of muck, to be drawn into
its mysteries, to breathe in all that
death as if it were a nosegay.

VIII

For another try…

So Far at Least

humans have not been able to stop the wind.
Oh, I know it can blow off roofs
and whomp up humongous, street-eating waves,
but, this hot June night, it merely tousles
the crown of the elm, ruffles ferns' feathers,
sends a tremble through all petals
and puts a sizzle into the leaves.
It keens through the newly-candled pines
for the home it will never know,
gives underwing boosts to the birds
and treats me like a love lost long,
stroking and stroking, as if in glad disbelief
at my return, my arms and my cheeks.
It cools the sweat now moist on my brow
and moans over my world's-end dreams.

Driving Toward New Milford, May 1

This green is gold, this
first of May fuzz
fluffed up on
the arched back of the town
like duckling's down, like
green-gold clouds shining
the trees. This must be
what eyes first see unwrapped
from a shroud. The cold,
dead dream of winter, where
everything folds – the houseplan,
the gig, walls of the aorta –
does not hold,
Spreading over the tops of
the trees like gooseflesh
is the prize hard won by
all our unlit hours:
this green, gold
that buys
a new chapter.

Wood Thrush

I

Sharp and clear
twinkling above
the palaver of other birds,
your call trills my dead center,
loosening clods for seeds.

II

You run this flat morning
through your pipes,
turning it, tuning it,
until it takes on depth and
opens as night does with dreams,
and I can breathe again –
an atmosphere of lilacs.

III

When, scarred
from years of leaf fall,
I think I can't go on, you,
singing like the spangling flash
at the end of a wand,
touch me and flesh me into a world
where pursed ends blossom
to extend their green
and azaleas
sear the air magenta.

IV

Sent over my hollows,
your song flutters
like the first spirit
to draw up stuff
from nothing,
wanting me, avidly
as you do those eggs
to crack open
freshly formed.

V

Where you come from
you would take me,
the big tree whose branches
are the Mother's arms
your flutes beckoning,
"Come with me,
Come with me home."

Again

In wet depressions, in gunk:
thrumming. Peepers
thumbing tines of electric combs,
idly strumming, to get green ideas
for waking
the peakèd, gone-blank ground.

Blackbirds swoop and churr
stirring and stirring
the embers in cold
fanning them so oak buds
get red as their epaulets.

The long suffering sun
raises from buried, left-for-dead
bulbs, rhizomes, roots
shoots cocked for flower.

The bar-tailed godwit
wings non-stop 9000 miles from Alaska
over the Pacific for a specific
New Zealand spot to nest,
in stuff it plucks, three golden eggs.

And, from a winter
that's left you stripped,
lop-limbed and limping,
if birches, bereft of every one
of their leaves keep thrusting
fingers to the heavens, higher
every year by only inches, can't you
from deep in your earth
summon sap for another try?

O Cyclamen,

your pink wings that spring from
a clutch of mottled green hearts
sing, pendant above them, of
dropped stars, splashing roseate into dusk.
Your fuchsine mouths
have kissed my quick and
bits of me, buds, leap up and
open out flame-like as
your reflexed petals
to heat this drafty February study,
while rain outside, that should be snow,
beats down every try, every hope.
                    Thank you.

Fewer

for PB & PC

There is a dwindling remnant
who, in April, make a daily pilgrimage
to the woods and can find nothing really
more agreeable than to come upon
a wild gobbler on the path fanning
his russet-striped tail feathers for a female,
younger males on the sidelines taking notes.
They *oooh* over the pink-veined blossoms
of spring beauties, trout lilies' mottled
greens beneath their yellow peeling out.
They can identify bloodroot and know,
if the leaves relax away from the stem,
their pure white blooming's done.
They can tell by the climb of the light
just when the water thrush will return
and case his hang outs – trickling creeks,
soggy ground, but, though they can hear him –
his call is loud – fear, because he is shy,
they might not live for the Spring they'd
lay eyes again on this old chum. For memory,
a "fall," maybe a hundred, of soft olive
palm warblers dropping down right before them
in a field suffices and consoles. Next to
a particular boulder, so many paces
down the trail, they're certain they remember,
by its sheltering heart-shaped leaves
and hairy stems, a spot where wild ginger sprouts,
concealing, in the stem's crotch, three passionate
red-brown, down-turned petals. Sure enough!
Call them appreciants, acolytes at the altar
of our overheating earth. Who's to say
these species aren't fading because there are fewer
of this tribe to prize them? As they depart, a clump
of marsh marigolds beams at them from the swamp.

Letting Go

The bodies of your dead
are too heavy to carry.
Nothing you can do
will redeem them.
Lay them down.
Drink the rain.
Root deep.
Burst like the nasturtium
whose stem bends
under star-shot green umbrellas.
The breeze incites its
silent flamenco.
If you refuse to release those
once close,
you will never expose
the tiny wild tentacles at your center,
you will never know
gamboge.
Once loose,
see how they are light as seed.
Sow them in the zenith,
darkness plowed by
spiralling galaxies,
to bloom, as here they could not have,
novas, out of universal loam.

About the Author

Susan Deborah King is the author of four previous collections of poetry including *Coven, One-Breasted Woman* and *Bog Orchids.* She teaches creative writing, leads retreats on creativity and spirituality, and divides her time between Minneapolis and an island off the coast of Maine.